Reflections

Verses from the Bahá'í Teachings

compiled by

Akwasi O. Osei

GEORGE RONALD
OXFORD

GEORGE RONALD, Publisher
46 High Street, Kidlington, Oxford OX5 2DN

ISBN 0-85398-386-0

A Cataloguing-in-Publication entry is available
from the British Library

Cover Painting by Chehreh Goodwin
Typeset by ComputerCraft, Knoxville, Tennessee, USA
Printed and bound in Great Britain by
Biddles Ltd, Guildford and King's Lynn

Contents

To Lovers of Wisdom

Reflections
on the Meaning of Life

The Purpose of Life

ALL MEN have been created to carry forward an ever-advancing civilization.[1]

THE WHOLE DUTY of man in this Day is to attain that share of the flood of grace which God poureth forth for him. Let none, therefore, consider the largeness or smallness of the receptacle. The portion of some might lie in the palm of a man's hand, the portion of others might fill a cup, and of others even a gallon-measure.[2]

GOD'S GRACE is like the rain that cometh down from heaven: the water is not bounded by the limitations of form, yet on whatever place it poureth down, it taketh on limitations – dimensions, appearance, shape – according to the characteristics of that place. In a square pool, the water, previously unconfined, becometh a square; in a six-sided pool it becometh a hexagon, in an eight-sided pool an octagon, and so forth. The rain itself hath no geometry, no limits, no form, but it taketh on one form or another, according to the restrictions of its vessel.[3]

Our True Nature

MAN IS THE supreme Talisman. Lack of a proper education hath, however, deprived him of that which he doth inherently possess. Through a word proceeding out of the mouth of God he was called into being; by one word more he was guided to recognize the Source of his education; by yet another word his station and destiny were safeguarded. The Great Being saith: Regard man as a mine rich in gems of inestimable value. Education can, alone, cause it to reveal its treasures, and enable mankind to benefit therefrom.[4]

THE REALITY of man is his thought, not his material body.[5]

WISDOM is the glory of man, not ignorance; light, not darkness![6]

. . . UNLESS the moral character of a nation is educated, as well as its brain and its talents, civilization has no sure basis.[7]

ONE FRUITFUL TREE will be conducive to the life of society, whereas a thousand forests of wild trees offer no fruits. The plain is covered with pebbles, but precious stones are rare. One pearl is better than a thousand wildernesses of sand. . .[8]

IF MAN were to care for himself only he would be nothing but an animal for only the animals are thus egoistic. If you bring a thousand sheep to a well to kill nine hundred and ninety-nine the one remaining sheep would go on grazing, not thinking of the others and worrying not at all about the lost, never bothering that its own kind had passed away, or had perished or been killed. To look after one's self only is therefore an animal propensity. It is the animal propensity to live solitary and alone. It is the animal proclivity to look after one's own comfort. But man was created to be a man – to be fair, to be just, to be merciful, to be kind to all his species, never to be willing that he himself be well off while others are in misery and distress – this is an attribute of the animal and not of man. Nay, rather, man should be willing to accept hardships for himself in order that others may enjoy wealth; he should enjoy trouble for himself that others may enjoy happiness and well-being. This is the attribute of man. This is becoming of man. Otherwise man is not man – he is less than the animal.

The man who thinks only of himself and is thoughtless of others is undoubtedly inferior to the animal because the animal is not possessed of the reasoning faculty. The animal is excused; but in man there is reason, the faculty of justice, the faculty of mercifulness.

Possessing all these faculties he must not leave them unused. He who is so hard-hearted as to think only of his own comfort, such an one will not be called man.[9]

MAN IS he who forgets his own interests for the sake of others. His own comfort he forfeits for the well-being of all. Nay, rather, his own life must he be willing to forfeit for the life of mankind. Such a man is the honour of the world of humanity. Such a man is the glory of the world of mankind. Such a man is the one who wins eternal bliss. Such a man is near to the threshold of God. Such a man is the very manifestation of eternal happiness. Otherwise, men are like animals, exhibiting the same proclivities and propensities as the world of animals. What distinction is there? What prerogatives, what perfections? None whatever! Animals are better even – thinking only of themselves and negligent of the needs of others.

Consider how the greatest men in the world – whether among prophets or philosophers – all have forfeited their own comfort, have sacrificed their own pleasure for the well-being of humanity. They have sacrificed their own lives for the body politic. They have sacrificed their own wealth for that of the general welfare. They have forfeited their own honour for the honour of mankind. Therefore it becomes evident that this is the highest attainment for the world of humanity.[10]

The Individual in Society

WE ARE the fruits of one tree, and the leaves of one branch.[11]

THAT ONE INDEED is a man who, today, dedicateth himself to the service of the entire human race.[12]

TODAY THERE IS no greater glory for man than that of service in the cause of the Most Great Peace.[13]

. . . IN A WORLD of inter-dependent peoples and nations the advantage of the part is best to be reached by the advantage of the whole, and . . . no abiding benefit can be conferred upon the component parts if the general interests of the entity itself are ignored or neglected.[14]

True Civilization

MATERIAL CIVILIZATION is like unto the lamp, while spiritual civilization is the light in that lamp. If the material and spiritual civilization become united, then we will have the light and the lamp together, and the outcome will be perfect. For material civilization is like unto a beautiful body, and spiritual civilization is like unto the spirit of life. If that wondrous spirit of life enters this beautiful body, the body will become a channel for the distribution and development of the perfections of humanity.[15]

The Golden Rule

BLESSED IS HE who preferreth his brother before himself.[16]

O SON of man! If thine eyes be turned towards mercy, forsake the things that profit thee and cleave unto that which will profit mankind. And if thine eyes be turned towards justice, choose thou for thy neighbour that which thou choosest for thyself. Humility exalteth man to the heaven of glory and power, whilst pride abaseth him to the depths of wretchedness and degradation.[17]

MAN HAS the power both to do good and to do evil; if his power for good predominates and his inclinations to do wrong are conquered, then man in truth may be called a saint. But if, on the contrary, he rejects the things of God and allows his evil passions to conquer him, then he is no better than a mere animal.[18]

Progress

K NOW THAT nothing which exists remains in a state of repose – that is to say, all things are in motion. Everything is either growing or declining; all things are either coming from nonexistence into being, or going from existence into nonexistence.[19]

YOU MUST ever press forward, never standing still; avoid stagnation, the first step to a backward movement, to decay.[20]

The Meaning of Suffering

LAMENT NOT in your hours of trial, neither rejoice therein; seek ye the Middle Way . . . [21]

O SON of Man! For everything there is a sign. The sign of love is fortitude under My decree and patience under My trials.[22]

THE MIND AND SPIRIT of man advance when he is tried by suffering. The more the ground is ploughed the better the seed will grow, the better the harvest will be. Just as the plough furrows the earth deeply, purifying it of weeds and thistles, so suffering and tribulation free man from the petty affairs of this worldly life until he arrives at a state of complete detachment. His attitude in this world will be that of divine happiness. Man is, so to speak, unripe: the heat of the fire of suffering will mature him. Look back to the times past and you will find that the greatest men have suffered most.[23]

THOSE WHO suffer most, attain to the greatest perfection.[24]

NOT UNTIL man is tried doth the pure gold distinctly separate from the dross. Torment is the fire of test wherein the pure gold shineth resplendently and the impurity is burned and blackened.[25]

LET THEM NEVER be defeated by the malice of the people, by their aggression and their hate, no matter how intense. If others hurl their darts against you, offer them milk and honey in return; if they poison your lives, sweeten their souls; if they injure you, teach them how to be comforted; if they inflict a wound upon you, be a balm to their sores; if they sting you, hold to their lips a refreshing cup.[26]

The Search for Truth

W HEN WE ARE in earnest in our search for anything we look for it everywhere.[27]

. . . MAN MUST BE the seeker after the Reality, and he will find that Reality in each of the Sanctified Souls. He must be fascinated and enraptured, and attracted to the divine bounty; he must be like the butterfly who is the lover of the light from whatever lamp it may shine, and like the nightingale who is the lover of the rose in whatever garden it may grow.[28]

THE STATE in which one should be to seriously search for the truth is the condition of the thirsty, burning soul desiring the water of life, of the fish struggling to reach the sea, of the sufferer seeking for the true doctor to obtain the divine cure, of the lost caravan endeavouring to find the right road, of the lost and wandering ship striving to reach the shore of salvation.

Therefore, the seeker must be endowed with certain qualities. First of all, he must be just and severed from all else save God; his heart must be entirely turned to the supreme horizon; he must be free from the bondage of self and passion, for all these are obstacles. Furthermore, he must be able to endure all hardships. He must be absolutely pure and sanctified, and free from the love or the hatred of the inhabitants of the world. Why? because the fact of his love for any person or thing might prevent him from recognizing the truth in another, and, in the same way, hatred for anything might be a hindrance in discerning truth. This is the condition of seeking, and the seeker must have these qualities and attributes. Until he reaches this condition, it is not possible for him to attain to the Sun of Reality.[29]

Sanctifying Oneself

O MY FRIEND in Word! Ponder awhile. Hast thou ever heard that friend and foe should abide in one heart? Cast out then the stranger, that the Friend may enter His home.[30]

SUFFER NOT your idle fancies, your evil passions, your insincerity and blindness of heart to dim the lustre, or stain the sanctity, of so lofty a station. Ye are even as the bird which soareth, with the full force of its mighty wings and with complete and joyous confidence, through the immensity of the heavens, until, impelled to satisfy its hunger, it turneth longingly to the water and clay of the earth below it, and, having been entrapped in the mesh of its desire, findeth itself impotent to resume its flight to the realms whence it came. Powerless to shake off the burden weighing on its sullied wings, that bird, hitherto an inmate of the heavens, is now forced to seek a dwelling-place upon the dust. Wherefore, O My servants, defile not your wings with the clay of waywardness and vain desires, and suffer them not to be stained with the dust of envy and hate, that ye may not be hindered from soaring in the heavens of My divine knowledge.[31]

Knowing Oneself

T RUE LOSS is for him whose days have been spent in utter ignorance of his self.[32]

. . . MAN SHOULD know his own self and recognize that which leadeth unto loftiness or lowliness, glory or abasement, wealth or poverty. Having attained the stage of fulfilment and reached his maturity, man standeth in need of wealth, and such wealth as he acquireth through crafts or professions is commendable and praiseworthy in the estimation of men of wisdom, and especially in the eyes of servants who dedicate themselves to the education of the world and to the edification of its peoples.[33]

A SEED in the beginning is very small, but in the end a great tree.[34]

Reflections
on the Mystery of Love

The Reality of Love

K NOW THOU of a certainty that Love is the secret of God's holy Dispensation, the manifestation of the All-Merciful, the fountain of spiritual outpourings. Love is heaven's kindly light, the Holy Spirit's eternal breath that vivifieth the human soul. Love is the cause of God's revelation unto man, the vital bond inherent, in accordance with the divine creation, in the realities of things. Love is the one means that ensureth true felicity both in this world and the next. Love is the light that guideth in darkness, the living link that uniteth God with man, that assureth the progress of every illumined soul. Love is the most great law that ruleth this mighty and heavenly cycle, the unique power that bindeth together the divers elements of this material world, the supreme magnetic force that directeth the movements of the spheres in the celestial realms. Love revealeth with unfailing and limitless power the mysteries latent in the universe. Love is the spirit of life unto the adorned body of mankind, the establisher of true civilization in this mortal world, and the shedder of imperishable glory upon every high-aiming race and nation.[35]

WE DECLARE that love is the cause of the existence of all phenomena and that the absence of love is the cause of disintegration or nonexistence. Love is the conscious bestowal of God, the bond of affiliation in all phenomena. We will first consider the proof of this through sense perception. As we look upon the universe, we observe that all composite beings or existing phenomena are made up primarily of single elements bound together by a power of attraction. Through this power of attraction cohesion has become manifest between atoms of these composing elements. The resultant being is a phenomenon of the lower contingent type. The power of cohesion expressed in the mineral kingdom is in reality love or affinity manifested in a low degree according to the exigencies of the mineral world. We take a step higher into the vegetable kingdom where we find an increased power of attraction has become manifest among the composing elements which form phenomena. Through this degree of attraction a cellular admixture is produced among these elements which make up the body of a plant. Therefore, in the degree of the vegetable kingdom there is love. We enter the animal kingdom and find the attractive power binding together single elements as in the mineral, plus the cellular admixture as in the vegetable, plus the phenomena of feelings or susceptibilities. We observe that the animals are susceptible to certain affiliation and fellowship and that they exercise natural selection. This elemental attraction, this admixture and selective affinity is love manifest in the degree of the animal kingdom.

Finally, we come to the kingdom of man. As this is the superior kingdom, the light of love is more resplendent. In man we find the power of attraction among the elements which compose his material body, plus the attraction which produces cellular admixture or augmentative power, plus the attraction which characterizes the sensibilities of the animal kingdom, but still beyond and above all these lower powers we discover in the being of man the attraction of heart, the susceptibilities and affinities which bind men together, enabling them to live and associate in friendship and solidarity. It is, therefore, evident that in the world of humanity the greatest king and sovereign is love. If love were extinguished, the power of attraction dispelled, the affinity of human hearts destroyed, the phenomena of human life would disappear.[36]

The Power of Love

T HE BRIGHTNESS of the fire of your love will no
doubt fuse and unify the contending peoples
and kindreds of the earth, whilst the fierceness
of the flame of enmity and hatred cannot but result in
strife and ruin.[37]

LOVE GIVES life to the lifeless. Love lights a flame in the
heart that is cold. Love brings hope to the hopeless and
gladdens the hearts of the sorrowful.[38]

THE CAUSE of the creation of the phenomenal world is
love.[39]

. . . THE AXIS around which life revolves is love, while the
axis around which death and destruction revolve is
animosity and hatred. Let us view the mineral kingdom.
Here we see that if attraction did not exist between the
atoms, the composite substance of matter would not be
possible. Every existent phenomenon is composed of
elements and cellular particles. This is scientifically true
and correct. If attraction did not exist between the
elements and among the cellular particles, the com-

position of that phenomenon would never have been possible. For instance, the stone is an existent phenomenon, a composition of elements. A bond of attraction has brought them together, and through this cohesion of ingredients this petrous object has been formed. This stone is the lowest degree of phenomena, but nevertheless within it a power of attraction is manifest without which the stone could not exist. This power of attraction in the mineral world is love, the only expression of love the stone can manifest.[40]

The True Lover

T HE TRUE SEEKER hunteth naught but the object of his quest, and the lover hath no desire save union with his beloved. Nor shall the seeker reach his goal unless he sacrifice all things.[41]

O SON of Justice! Whither can a lover go but to the land of his beloved? and what seeker findeth rest away from his heart's desire? To the true lover reunion is life, and separation is death. His breast is void of patience and his heart hath no peace. A myriad lives he would forsake to hasten to the abode of his beloved.[42]

DOTH IT BESEEM a lover to flee from his beloved, or to desert the object of his heart's desire?[43]

WHEN THE HEART of man is aglow with the flame of love, he is ready to sacrifice all – even his life.[44]

THE GREATEST HAPPINESS for a lover is to converse with his beloved, and the greatest gift for a seeker is to become familiar with the object of his longing . . .[45]

The Madness of Love

LOVE ACCEPTETH no existence and wisheth no life: He seeth life in death, and in shame seeketh glory. To merit the madness of love, man must abound in sanity . . .[46]

. . . WHEN THE FIRE of love is ablaze, it burneth to ashes the harvest of reason.[47]

THE LEVIATHAN OF LOVE swalloweth the master of reason and destroyeth the lord of knowledge.[48]

. . . YEA, PHYSICIANS have no medicine for one sick of love, unless the favour of the beloved one deliver him.[49]

Love of Humanity

T HEY THAT are endued with sincerity and faithfulness should associate with all the peoples and kindreds of the earth with joy and radiance, inasmuch as consorting with people hath promoted and will continue to promote unity and concord, which in turn are conducive to the maintenance of order in the world and to the regeneration of nations. Blessed are such as hold fast to the cord of kindliness and tender mercy and are free from animosity and hatred.[50]

BE VIGILANT, that ye may not do injustice to anyone, be it to the extent of a grain of mustard seed. Tread ye the path of justice, for this, verily, is the straight path.[51]

THE TABERNACLE of Unity hath been raised; regard ye not one another as strangers . . .[52]

O FRIEND! In the garden of thy heart plant naught but the rose of love, and from the nightingale of affection and desire loosen not thy hold. Treasure the companionship of the righteous and eschew all fellowship with the ungodly.[53]

IF YOU DESIRE with all your heart, friendship with every race on earth, your thought, spiritual and positive, will spread; it will become the desire of others, growing stronger and stronger, until it reaches the minds of all men.[54]

THE DIVERSITY in the human family should be the cause of love and harmony, as it is in music where many different notes blend together in the making of a perfect chord.[55]

LOVE IS LIGHT in whatsoever house it may shine and enmity is darkness in whatsoever abode it dwell.[56]

IF LOVE and agreement are manifest in a single family, that family will advance, become illumined and spiritual; but if enmity and hatred exist within it, destruction and dispersion are inevitable. This is, likewise, true of a city. If those who dwell within it manifest a spirit of accord and fellowship, it will progress steadily and human conditions become brighter, whereas through enmity and strife it will be degraded and its inhabitants scattered. In the same way, the people of a nation develop and advance toward civilization and enlightenment through love and accord and are disintegrated by war and strife. Finally, this is true of humanity itself in the aggregate. When love is realized and the ideal spiritual bonds unite the hearts of men, the whole human race will be uplifted, the world will continually grow more spiritual and radiant and the happiness and tranquillity of mankind be immeasurably increased. Warfare and strife will be uprooted, disagreement and dissension pass away and universal peace unite the nations and peoples of the world. All mankind will dwell together as one family, blend as the waves of one sea, shine as stars of one firmament and appear as fruits of the same tree. This is the happiness and felicity of humankind. This is the illumination of man, the eternal glory and everlasting life; this is the divine bestowal.[57]

BROTHERHOOD, or fraternity, is of different kinds. It may be family association, the intimate relationship of the household. This is limited and subject to change and disruption. How often it happens that in a family love and agreement are changed into enmity and antagonism. Another form of fraternity is manifest in patriotism. Man loves his fellowmen because they belong to the same native land. This is also limited and subject to change and disintegration as, for instance, when sons of the same fatherland are opposed to each other in war, bloodshed and battle. Still another brotherhood, or fraternity, is that which arises from racial unity, the oneness of racial origin, producing ties of affinity and association. This, likewise, has its limitation and liability to change, for often war and deadly strife have been witnessed between people and nations of the same racial lineage. There is a fourth kind of brotherhood, the attitude of man toward humanity itself, the altruistic love of humankind and recognition of the fundamental human bond.[58]

BE KIND to all peoples and nations, have love for all of them, exert yourselves to purify the hearts as much as you can, and bestow abundant effort in rejoicing the souls. Be ye a sprinkling of rain to every meadow and a water of life to every tree. Be ye as fragrant musk to every nostril and a soul-refreshing breeze to every invalid. Be ye salutary water to every thirsty one, a wise guide to every one led astray, an affectionate father or mother to every orphan, and, in the utmost joy and fragrance, a son or daughter to every one bent with age. Be ye a rich treasure to every indigent one; consider love and union as a delectable paradise, and count annoyance and hostility as the torment of hell-fire.[59]

BE YE loving fathers to the orphan, and a refuge to the helpless, and a treasury for the poor, and a cure for the ailing. Be ye the helpers of every victim of oppression, the patrons of the disadvantaged. Think ye at all times of rendering some service to every member of the human race. Pay ye no heed to aversion and rejection, to disdain, hostility, injustice: act ye in the opposite way. Be ye sincerely kind, not in appearance only. Let each one of God's loved ones centre his attention on this: to be the Lord's mercy to man; to be the Lord's grace. Let him do some good to every person whose path he crosseth, and be of some benefit to him.[60]

. . . MAY EACH ONE of you be even as a candle casting its light, the centre of attraction wherever people come together; and from you, as from a bed of flowers, may sweet scents be shed.[61]

YE ARE the fruits of one tree and the leaves of one branch; be ye compassionate and kind to all the human race. Deal ye with strangers the same as with friends, cherish ye others just as ye would your own. See foes as friends; see demons as angels; give to the tyrant the same great love ye show the loyal and true, and even as gazelles from the scented cities of Khatá and Khutan offer up sweet musk to the ravening wolf. Be ye a refuge to the fearful; bring ye rest and peace to the disturbed; make ye a provision for the destitute; be a treasury of riches for the poor; be a healing medicine for those who suffer pain; be ye doctor and nurse to the ailing; promote ye friendship, and honour, and conciliation, and devotion to God, in this world of non-existence.[62]

ENKINDLE with all your might in every meeting the light of the love of God, gladden and cheer every heart with the utmost loving-kindness, show forth your love to the strangers just as you show forth to your relations. If a soul is seeking to quarrel, ask ye for reconciliation; if he blame you, praise him; if he give you a deadly poison, bestow ye an all-healing antidote; if he createth death, administer ye eternal life; if he becometh a thorn, change ye into roses and hyacinths. Perchance, through such deeds and words, this darkened world will become illuminated, this terrestrial universe will become transformed into a heavenly realm, and this satanic prison become a divine court; warfare and bloodshed be annihilated, and love and faithfulness hoist the tent of unity upon the apex of the world.[63]

Reflections
on Peace

The Futility of War

BEHOLD the disturbances which, for many a long year, have afflicted the earth, and the perturbation that hath seized its peoples. It hath either been ravaged by war, or tormented by sudden and unforeseen calamities. Though the world is encompassed with misery and distress, yet no man hath paused to reflect what the cause or source of that may be. Whenever the True Counsellor uttered a word in admonishment, lo, they all denounced Him as a mover of mischief and rejected His claim. How bewildering, how confusing is such behaviour! No two men can be found who may be said to be outwardly and inwardly united. The evidences of discord and malice are apparent everywhere, though all were made for harmony and union. The Great Being saith: O well-beloved ones! The tabernacle of unity hath been raised; regard ye not one another as strangers. Ye are the fruits of one tree, and the leaves of one branch.[64]

STRIFE LEADS to bloodshed and provokes commotion amongst people.[65]

. . . FOR A FEW DAYS we live on this earth and eventually we are buried in it, it is our eternal tomb. Is it worth while that we should engage in bloodshed and tear one another to pieces for this eternal tomb?[66]

THE DOMESTIC ANIMALS do not manifest hatred and cruelty toward each other; that is the attribute of the wild and ferocious beasts. In a flock of one thousand sheep you will witness no bloodshed. Numberless species of birds are peaceful in flocks. Wolves, lions, tigers are ferocious because it is their natural and necessary means for obtaining food. Man has no need of such ferocity; his food is provided in other ways. Therefore, it is evident that warfare, cruelty and bloodshed in the kingdom of man are caused by human greed, hatred and selfishness. The kings and rulers of nations enjoy luxury and ease in their palaces and send the common people to the battlefield – offer them as the food and targets of cannon. Each day they invent new instruments for the more complete destruction of the foundations of the human race. They are callous and merciless toward their fellow creatures. What shall atone for the sufferings and grief of mothers who have so tenderly cared for their sons? What sleepless nights they have spent, and what days of devotion and love they have given to bring their children to maturity! Yet the savagery of these warring rulers causes great numbers of their victims to be torn and mutilated in a day. What ignorance and degradation, yea even greater than the ferocious beasts themselves! For a wolf will carry away and devour one sheep at a time, whereas an ambitious tyrant may cause the death of one hundred thousand men in a battle and glory in his military prowess, saying, 'I am commander in chief; I have won this mighty victory.' Consider the ignorance and inconsistency of the human race. If a man kills another, no matter what the cause may be, he is pronounced a murderer, imprisoned or executed; but the brutal oppressor who has slain one hundred thousand is idolized as a hero, conqueror or military genius. A man steals a small sum of money; he is called a thief and sent to the penitentiary; but the military leader who invades and pillages a whole kingdom is acclaimed heroic and a mighty man of valour. How base and ignorant is man![67]

GOVERNMENTS . . . consider militarism as the step to human progress, that division among men and nations is the cause of patriotism and honour, that if one nation attack and conquer another, gaining wealth, territory and glory thereby, this warfare and conquest, this bloodshed and cruelty are the cause of that victorious nation's advancement and prosperity. This is an utter mistake. Compare the nations of the world to the members of a family. A family is a nation in miniature. Simply enlarge the circle of the household, and you have the nation. Enlarge the circle of nations, and you have all humanity. The conditions surrounding the family surround the nation. The happenings in the family are the happenings in the life of the nation. Would it add to the progress and advancement of a family if dissensions should arise among its members, all fighting, pillaging each other, jealous and revengeful of injury, seeking selfish advantage? Nay, this would be the cause of the effacement of progress and advancement. So it is in the great family of nations, for nations are but an aggregate of families. Therefore, as strife and dissension destroy a family and prevent its progress, so nations are destroyed and advancement hindered.[68]

THERE IS NOTHING so heart-breaking and terrible as an outburst of human savagery![69]

TYRANNY has ever sought to overcome justice. Ignorance has persistently tried to trample knowledge under foot. This has, from the earliest ages, been the method of the material world.[70]

THE CONQUEROR shall one day be conquered; and the vanquished ones victorious![71]

THIS RECENT WAR has proved to the world and the people that war is destruction while Universal Peace is construction; war is death while peace is life; war is rapacity and bloodthirstiness while peace is beneficence and humaneness; war is an appurtenance of the world of nature while peace is of the foundation of the religion of God; war is darkness upon darkness while peace is heavenly light; war is the destroyer of the edifice of mankind while peace is the everlasting life of the world of humanity; war is like a devouring wolf while peace is like the angels of heaven; war is the struggle for existence while peace is mutual aid and cooperation among the peoples of the world and the cause of the good-pleasure of the True One in the heavenly realm.

There is not one soul whose conscience does not testify that in this day there is no more important matter in the world than that of Universal Peace. Every just one bears witness to this . . . [the] aim is that this darkness may be changed into light, this bloodthirstiness into kindness, this torment into bliss, this hardship into ease and this enmity and hatred into fellowship and love.[72]

. . . THE FIRE OF WAR is world-consuming, whereas the rays of peace are world-enlightening. One is death, the other is life; this is extinction, that is immortality; one is the most great calamity, the other is the most great bounty; this is darkness, that is light; this is eternal humiliation and that is everlasting glory; one is the destroyer of the foundation of man, the other is the founder of the prosperity of the human race.[73]

The Value of Peace

PEACE IS LIGHT, whereas war is darkness. Peace is life; war is death. Peace is guidance; war is error. Peace is the foundation of God; war is a satanic institution. Peace is the illumination of the world of humanity; war is the destroyer of human foundations. When we consider outcomes in the world of existence, we find that peace and fellowship are factors of upbuilding and betterment, whereas war and strife are the causes of destruction and disintegration. All created things are expressions of the affinity and cohesion of elementary substances, and nonexistence is the absence of their attraction and agreement. Various elements unite harmoniously in composition, but when these elements become discordant, repelling each other, decomposition and nonexistence result. Everything partakes of this nature and is subject to this principle, for the creative foundation in all its degrees and kingdoms is an expression or outcome of love. Consider the restlessness and agitation of the human world today because of war. Peace is health and construction; war is disease and dissolution. When the banner of truth is raised, peace becomes the cause of the welfare and advancement of the human world.[74]

... THAT CONFLICT and aggression might be put to flight, the lance and the keen blade be exchanged for loving fellowship, malevolence and war turn into safety and gentleness and love, that battlefields of hate and wrath should become gardens of delight, and places where once the blood-drenched armies clashed, be fragrant pleasure grounds; that warfare should be seen as shame, and the resort to arms, even as a loathsome sickness, be shunned by every people; that universal peace raise its pavilions on the loftiest mounts, and war be made to perish forever from the earth.[75]

Obstacles to Peace

PREJUDICES of any kind are the destroyers of human happiness and welfare. Until they are dispelled the advancement of the world of humanity is not possible, yet racial, religious and national bias are observed everywhere. For thousands of years the world of humanity has been agitated and disturbed by prejudices. As long as it prevails, warfare, animosity and hatred will continue. Therefore if we seek to establish peace we must cast aside this obstacle, for otherwise agreement and composure are not to be attained.[76]

How to Achieve Peace

BEWARE LEST ye sow tares of dissension among men or plant thorns of doubt in pure and radiant hearts.

O ye beloved of the Lord! Commit not that which defileth the limpid stream of love or destroyeth the sweet fragrance of friendship. By the righteousness of the Lord! Ye were created to show love one to another and not perversity and rancour. Take pride not in love for yourselves but in love for your fellow-creatures. Glory not in love for your country, but in love for all mankind. Let your eye be chaste, your hand faithful, your tongue truthful and your heart enlightened. Abase not the station of the learned in Bahá and belittle not the rank of such rulers as administer justice amidst you. Set your reliance on the army of justice, put on the armour of wisdom, let your adorning be forgiveness and mercy . . .[77]

IT IS INCUMBENT upon all the peoples of the world to reconcile their differences, and, with perfect unity and peace, abide beneath the shadow of the Tree of His care and loving-kindness. It behoveth them to cleave to whatsoever will, in this Day, be conducive to the exaltation of their stations, and to the promotion of their best interests. Happy are those whom the all-glorious Pen was moved to remember, and blessed are those men whose names, by virtue of Our inscrutable decree, We have preferred to conceal.[78]

. . . CONCENTRATE all the thoughts of your heart on love and unity. When a thought of war comes, oppose it by a stronger thought of peace. A thought of hatred must be destroyed by a more powerful thought of love. Thoughts of war bring destruction to all harmony, well-being, restfulness and content.

Thoughts of love are constructive of brotherhood, peace, friendship, and happiness.[79]

THIS DAY, in the world of humanity, men are all the time expending, for war is nothing but the consumption of men and of wealth. At least engage ye in a deed of profit to the world of humanity that ye may partially compensate for that loss.[80]

WHEN LOVE is realized and the ideal spiritual bonds unite the hearts of men, the whole human race will be uplifted, the world will continually grow more spiritual and radiant and the happiness and tranquillity of mankind be immeasurably increased. Warfare and strife will be uprooted, disagreement and dissension pass away and Universal Peace unite the nations and peoples of the world. All mankind will dwell together as one family, blend as the waves of one sea, shine as stars of one firmament and appear as fruits of the same tree. This is the happiness and felicity of humankind. This is the illumination of man, the glory eternal and life everlasting; this is the divine bestowal.[81]

. . . IT IS OUR DUTY to put forth our greatest efforts and summon all our energies in order that the bonds of unity and accord may be established among mankind. For thousands of years we have had bloodshed and strife. It is enough; it is sufficient. Now is the time to associate together in love and harmony. For thousands of years we have tried the sword and warfare; let mankind for a time at least live in peace.[82]

THE HEARTS should be purified and cleansed from every trace of hatred and rancor and enabled to engage in truthfulness, conciliation, uprightness and love toward the world of humanity; so that the East and the West may embrace each other like unto two lovers, enmity and animosity may vanish from the human world and the universal peace be established![83]

. . . USE YOUR UNDERSTANDING to promote the unity and tranquillity of mankind, to give enlightenment and civilization to the people, to produce love in all around you, and to bring about the universal peace.[84]

USE YOUR KNOWLEDGE always for the benefit of others; so may war cease on the face of this beautiful earth, and a glorious edifice of peace and concord be raised.[85]

ALAS! WE SEE on all sides how cruel, prejudiced and unjust is man . . . If these people would love and help one another instead of being so eager to destroy with sword and cannon, how much nobler would it be! How much better if they would live like a flock of doves in peace and harmony, instead of being like wolves and tearing each other to pieces.[86]

BE THOU a summoner to love, and be thou kind to all the human race. Love thou the children of men and share in their sorrows. Be thou of those who foster peace. Offer thy friendship, be worthy of trust. Be thou a balm to every sore, be thou a medicine for every ill. Bind thou the souls together.[87]

Achieving Peace through Unity

B E YE as the fingers of one hand, the members of one body.[88]

O CONTENDING PEOPLES and kindreds of the earth! Set your faces towards unity, and let the radiance of its light shine upon you. Gather ye together, and for the sake of God resolve to root out whatever is the source of contention amongst you. Then will the effulgence of the world's great Luminary envelop the whole earth, and its inhabitants become the citizens of one city, and the occupants of one and the same throne. This wronged One hath, ever since the early days of His life, cherished none other desire but this, and will continue to entertain no wish except this wish. There can be no doubt whatever that the peoples of the world, of whatever race or religion, derive their inspiration from one heavenly Source, and are the subjects of one God. The difference between the ordinances under which they abide should be attributed to the varying requirements and exigencies of the age in which they were revealed. All of them, except a few which are the outcome of human perversity, were ordained of God, and are a reflection of

His Will and Purpose. Arise and, armed with the power of faith, shatter to pieces the gods of your vain imaginings, the sowers of dissension amongst you. Cleave unto that which draweth you together and uniteth you.[89]

WHEN YOU ENTER a rose-garden the wealth of colour and variety of floral forms spread before you a picture of wonder and beauty. The world of humanity is like a garden and the various races are the flowers which constitute its adornment and decoration. In the animal kingdom also we find variety of colour. See how the doves differ in beauty yet they live together in perfect peace, and love each other. They do not make difference of colour a cause of discord and strife. They view each other as the same species and kind. They know they are one in kind. Often a white dove soars aloft with a black one. Throughout the animal kingdom we do not find the creatures separated because of colour. They recognize unity of species and oneness of kind. If we do not find colour distinction drawn in a kingdom of lower intelligence and reason, how can it be justified among human beings, especially when we know that all have come from the same source and belong to the same household? In origin and intention of creation mankind is one. Distinctions of race and colour have arisen afterward.[90]

REVIEW HISTORY and consider how much savagery, how much bloodshed and battle the world has witnessed. It has been either religious warfare, political warfare or some other clash of human interests. The world of humanity has never enjoyed the blessing of universal

46

peace. Year by year the implements of warfare have been increased and perfected. Consider the wars of past centuries; only ten, fifteen or twenty thousand at the most were killed, but now it is possible to kill one hundred thousand in a single day. In ancient times warfare was carried on with the sword; today it is the smokeless gun. Formerly, battleships were sailing vessels; today they are dreadnoughts. Consider the increase and improvement in the weapons of war. God has created us all human, and all countries of the world are parts of the same globe. We are all His servants. He is kind and just to all. Why should we be unkind and unjust to each other? He provides for all. Why should we deprive one another? He protects and preserves all. Why should we kill our fellow creatures? If this warfare and strife be for the sake of religion, it is evident that it violates the spirit and basis of all religion. All the divine Manifestations have proclaimed the oneness of God and the unity of mankind. They have taught that men should love and mutually help each other in order that they might progress. Now if this conception of religion be true, its essential principle is the oneness of humanity. The fundamental truth of the Manifestations is peace. This underlies all religion, all justice. The divine purpose is that men should live in unity, concord and agreement and should love one another.[91]

. . . THE REAL and ultimate unity of mankind . . . will bring forth marvellous results. It will reconcile all religions, make warring nations loving, cause hostile kings to become friendly and bring peace and happiness to the human world. It will cement together the Orient and

Occident, remove forever the foundations of war and upraise the ensign of the Most Great Peace. These limited unities are therefore signs of that great unity which will make all the human family one by being productive of the attractions of conscience in mankind.[92]

IF THE ONENESS of the human world were established, all the differences which separate mankind would be eradicated. Strife and warfare would cease, and the world of humanity would find repose. Universal peace would be promoted, and the East and West would be conjoined in a strong bond. All men would be sheltered beneath one tabernacle. Native lands would become one; races and religions would be unified. The people of the world would live together in harmony, and their well-being would be assured.[93]

The Responsibility of the World's Rulers

WE SEE YOU increasing every year your expenditures, and laying the burden thereof on your subjects. This, verily, is wholly and grossly unjust. Fear the sighs and tears of this wronged One, and lay not excessive burdens on your peoples. Do not rob them to rear palaces for yourselves; nay rather choose for them that which ye choose for yourselves. Thus We unfold to your eyes that which profiteth you, if ye but perceive. Your people are your treasures. Beware lest your rule violate the commandments of God, and ye deliver your wards to the hands of the robber. By them ye rule, by their means ye subsist, by their aid ye conquer. Yet, how disdainfully ye look upon them! How strange, how very strange!

Now that ye have refused the Most Great Peace, hold ye fast unto this, the Lesser Peace, that haply ye may in some degree better your own condition and that of your dependents.

O rulers of the earth! Be reconciled among yourselves, that ye may need no more armaments save in a measure to safeguard your territories and dominions. Beware lest ye disregard the counsel of the All-Knowing, the Faithful.

Be united, O kings of the earth, for thereby will the tempest of discord be stilled amongst you, and your peoples find rest, if ye be of them that comprehend. Should any one among you take up arms against another, rise ye all against him, for this is naught but manifest justice.[94]

TODAY, THE TASK befitting great rulers is to establish universal peace, for in this lies the freedom of all peoples.[95]

TRUE CIVILIZATION will unfurl its banner in the midmost heart of the world whenever a certain number of its distinguished and high-minded sovereigns – the shining exemplars of devotion and determination – shall, for the good and happiness of all mankind, arise, with firm resolve and clear vision, to establish the Cause of Universal Peace. They must make the Cause of Peace the object of general consultation, and seek by every means in their power to establish a Union of the nations of the world. They must conclude a binding treaty and establish a covenant, the provisions of which shall be sound, inviolable and definite. They must proclaim it to all the world and obtain for it the sanction of all the human race. This supreme and noble undertaking – the real source of the peace and well-being of all the world – should be regarded as sacred by all that dwell on earth. All the forces of humanity must be mobilized to ensure the stability and permanence of this Most Great

Covenant. In this all-embracing Pact the limits and frontiers of each and every nation should be clearly fixed, the principles underlying the relations of governments towards one another definitely laid down, and all international agreements and obligations ascertained. In like manner, the size of the armaments of every government should be strictly limited, for if the preparations for war and the military forces of any nation should be allowed to increase, they will arouse the suspicion of others. The fundamental principle underlying this solemn Pact should be so fixed that if any government later violate any one of its provisions, all the governments on earth should arise to reduce it to utter submission, nay the human race as a whole should resolve, with every power at its disposal, to destroy that government. Should this greatest of all remedies be applied to the sick body of the world, it will assuredly recover from its ills and will remain eternally safe and secure.

Observe that if such a happy situation be forthcoming, no government would need continually to pile up the weapons of war, nor feel itself obliged to produce ever new military weapons with which to conquer the human race. A small force for the purposes of internal security, the correction of criminal and disorderly elements and the prevention of local disturbances, would be required – no more. In this way the entire population would, first of all, be relieved of the crushing burden of expenditure currently imposed for military purposes, and secondly, great numbers of people would cease to devote their time to the continual devising of new weapons of destruction – those testimonials of greed and

bloodthirstiness, so inconsistent with the gift of life –
and would instead bend their efforts to the production
of whatever will foster human existence and peace and
well-being, and would become the cause of universal
development and prosperity. Then every nation on
earth will reign in honour, and every people will be
cradled in tranquillity and content.[96]

Reflections
on Virtue

The Value of Being Virtuous

THE LIGHT of a good character surpasseth the light of the sun and the radiance thereof.[97]

MAN IS LIKE unto a tree. If he be adorned with fruit, he hath been and will ever be worthy of praise and commendation. Otherwise a fruitless tree is but fit for fire. The fruits of the human tree are exquisite, highly desired and dearly cherished. Among them are upright character, virtuous deeds and a goodly utterance. The springtime for earthly trees occurreth once every year, while the one for human trees appeareth in the Days of God – exalted be His glory. Were the trees of men's lives to be adorned in this divine Springtime with the fruits that have been mentioned, the effulgence of the light of Justice would, of a certainty, illumine all the dwellers of the earth and everyone would abide in tranquillity and contentment beneath the sheltering shadow of Him Who is the Object of all mankind. The Water for these trees is the living water of the sacred Words uttered by the Beloved of the world. In one instant are such trees planted and in the next their branches shall, through the outpourings of the showers of divine mercy, have reached the skies. A dried-up tree, however, hath never been nor will be worthy of any mention.[98]

VERILY, it is better a thousand times for a man to die than to continue living without virtue.

We have eyes wherewith to see, but if we do not use them how do they profit us? We have ears wherewith to hear, but if we are deaf of what use are they?[99]

BUT THE SPIRIT of man has two aspects: one divine, one satanic – that is to say, it is capable of the utmost perfection, or it is capable of the utmost imperfection. If it acquires virtues, it is the most noble of the existing beings; and if it acquires vices, it becomes the most degraded existence.[100]

Becoming Virtuous

O SON of Spirit! My first counsel is this: Possess a pure, kindly and radiant heart, that thine may be a sovereignty ancient, imperishable and everlasting.[101]

BE GENEROUS in prosperity, and thankful in adversity. Be worthy of the trust of thy neighbour, and look upon him with a bright and friendly face. Be a treasure to the poor, an admonisher to the rich, an answerer of the cry of the needy, a preserver of the sanctity of thy pledge. Be fair in thy judgement, and guarded in thy speech. Be unjust to no man, and show all meekness to all men. Be as a lamp unto them that walk in darkness, a joy to the sorrowful, a sea for the thirsty, a haven for the distressed, an upholder and defender of the victim of oppression. Let integrity and uprightness distinguish all thine acts. Be a home for the stranger, a balm to the suffering, a tower of strength for the fugitive. Be eyes to the blind, and a guiding light unto the feet of the erring. Be an ornament to the countenance of truth, a crown to the brow of fidelity, a pillar of the temple of righteousness, a breath of life to the body of mankind, an ensign of the hosts of justice, a luminary above the horizon of virtue, a dew to the soil of the human heart, an ark on the ocean of knowledge, a sun in the heaven of bounty, a gem on the diadem of wisdom, a shining light in the firmament of thy generation, a fruit upon the tree of humility.[102]

MAKE HASTE to love! Make haste to trust! Make haste to give! To guidance come![103]

IN THE MEETING PLACE of life be ye a guiding candle; in the skies of this world be dazzling stars; in the gardens of unity be birds of the spirit, singing of inner truths and mysteries.[104]

THE LIGHT of the sun becomes apparent in each object according to the capacity of that object. The difference is simply one of degree and receptivity. The stone would be a recipient only to a limited extent; another created thing might be as a mirror wherein the sun is fully reflected; but the same light shines upon both.

The most important thing is to polish the mirrors of hearts in order that they may become illumined and receptive of the divine light. One heart may possess the capacity of the polished mirror; another, be covered and obscured by the dust and dross of this world. Although the same Sun is shining upon both, in the mirror which is polished, pure and sanctified you may behold the Sun in all its fullness, glory and power, revealing its majesty and effulgence; but in the mirror which is rusted and obscured there is no capacity for reflection, although so far as the Sun itself is concerned it is shining thereon and is neither lessened nor deprived. Therefore, our duty lies in seeking to polish the mirrors of our hearts in order that we shall become reflectors of that light and recipients of the divine bounties which may be fully revealed through them.[105]

TO EVERY MEADOW be a shower of grace, to every tree the water of life; be as sweet musk to the sense of humankind, and to the ailing be a fresh, restoring breeze. Be pleasing waters to all those who thirst, a careful guide to all who have lost their way; be father and mother to the orphan, be loving sons and daughters to the old, be an abundant treasure to the poor. Think ye of love and good fellowship as the delights of heaven, think ye of hostility and hatred as the torments of hell.[106]

Virtues Befitting Our Dignity

O ACT like the beasts of the field is unworthy of man. Those virtues that befit his dignity are forbearance, mercy, compassion and loving-kindness towards all the peoples and kindreds of the earth.[107]

Courtesy

O PEOPLE of God! I admonish you to observe courtesy, for above all else it is the prince of virtues. Well is it with him who is illumined with the light of courtesy and is attired with the vesture of uprightness. Whoso is endued with courtesy hath indeed attained a sublime station.[108]

COURTESY, is, in truth, a raiment which fitteth all men, whether young or old. Well is it with him that adorneth his temple therewith, and woe unto him who is deprived of this great bounty.[109]

Detachment

NO MAN shall attain the shores of the ocean of true understanding except he be detached from all that is in heaven and on earth.[110]

. . . THE WORLD of nature is an animal world. Until man is born again from the world of nature, that is to say, becomes detached from the world of nature, he is essentially an animal . . .[111]

OUR GREATEST EFFORTS must be directed towards detachment from the things of the world; we must strive to become more spiritual, more luminous, to follow the counsel of the Divine Teaching, to serve the cause of unity and true equality, to be merciful, to reflect the love of the Highest on all men, so that the light of the Spirit shall be apparent in all our deeds, to the end that all humanity shall be united, the stormy sea thereof calmed, and all rough waves disappear from off the surface of life's ocean henceforth unruffled and peaceful.[112]

Equity

. . . EQUITY is the most fundamental among human virtues. The evaluation of all things must needs depend upon it.[113]

SAY: OBSERVE EQUITY in your judgement, ye men of understanding heart! He that is unjust in his judgement is destitute of the characteristics that distinguish man's station.[114]

Generosity

THE MAGNANIMITY of man must be heavenly or, in other words, it must be assisted by the divine confirmation, so that he may become the cause of the illumination of the world of humanity.[115]

Gentleness

UNLESS ye must,
Bruise not the serpent in the dust,
How much less wound a man.
And if ye can,
No ant should ye alarm,
Much less a brother harm.[116]

Humility

BLESSED ARE THE LEARNED that pride not themselves on
their attainments; and well is it with the righteous that
mock not the sinful, but rather conceal their misdeeds,
so that their own shortcomings may remain veiled to
men's eyes.[117]

Justice

O SON of Spirit! The best beloved of all things in My
sight is Justice; turn not away therefrom if thou desirest
Me, and neglect it not that I may confide in thee. By its
aid thou shalt see with thine own eyes and not through
the eyes of others, and shalt know of thine own knowledge and not through the knowledge of thy neighbour.
Ponder this in thy heart; how it behoveth thee to be.
Verily justice is My gift to thee and the sign of My
loving-kindness. Set it then before thine eyes.[118]

Knowledge

KNOWLEDGE is identical with guidance, and ignorance
is real error.

Happy are those who spend their days in gaining knowledge, in discovering the secrets of nature, and in penetrating the subtleties of pure truth! Woe to those who are contented with ignorance, whose hearts are gladdened by thoughtless imitation, who have fallen into the lowest depths of ignorance and foolishness, and who have wasted their lives![119]

EDUCATION makes the ignorant wise, the tyrant just, promotes happiness, strengthens the mind, develops the will and makes fruitless trees of humanity fruitful. Therefore, in the human world some have attained lofty degrees, while others grope in the abyss of despair. Nevertheless, the highest attainment is possible for every member of the human race even to the station of the Prophets.[120]

Moderation

HUMAN UTTERANCE is an essence which aspireth to exert its influence and needeth moderation. As to its influence, this is conditional upon refinement which in turn is dependent upon hearts which are detached and pure. As to its moderation, this hath to be combined with tact and wisdom . . .[121]

Reflection

THE SOURCE of crafts, sciences and arts is the power of reflection. Make ye every effort that out of this ideal mine there may gleam forth such pearls of wisdom and utterance as will promote the well-being and harmony of all the kindreds of the earth.[122]

Trustworthiness

TRUSTWORTHINESS is the greatest portal leading unto the tranquillity and security of the people. In truth the stability of every affair hath depended and doth depend upon it. All the domains of power, of grandeur and of wealth are illumined by its light.[123]

Truthfulness

FAIR SPEECH and truthfulness, by reason of their lofty rank and position, are regarded as a sun shining above the horizon of knowledge.[124]

THE INDIVIDUAL must be educated to such a high degree that he would rather have his throat cut than tell a lie, and would think it easier to be slashed with a sword or pierced with a spear than to utter calumny or be carried away by wrath.

Thus will be kindled the sense of human dignity and pride, to burn away the reapings of lustful appetites.[125]

Wisdom

KNOW THOU that they who are truly wise have likened the world unto the human temple. As the body of man needeth a garment to clothe it, so the body of mankind must needs be adorned with the mantle of justice and wisdom.[126]

ABOVE ALL ELSE, the greatest gift and the most wondrous blessing hath ever been and will continue to be Wisdom. It is man's unfailing Protector. It aideth him and strengtheneth him. Wisdom is God's Emissary and the Revealer of His Name the Omniscient. Through it the loftiness of man's station is made manifest and evident. It is all-knowing and the foremost Teacher in the school of existence. It is the Guide and is invested with high distinction. Thanks to its educating influence earthly beings have become imbued with a gem-like spirit which outshineth the heavens.[127]

THE MAN of consummate learning and the sage endowed with penetrating wisdom are the two eyes to the body of mankind.[128]

O SON of Dust! The wise are they that speak not unless they obtain a hearing, even as the cup-bearer, who proffereth not his cup till he findeth a seeker, and the lover who crieth not out from the depths of his heart until he gazeth upon the beauty of his beloved. Wherefore sow the seeds of wisdom and knowledge in the pure soil of the heart, and keep them hidden, till the hyacinths of divine wisdom spring from the heart and not from mire and clay.[129]

Suffering Develops Virtue

T HE LABOURER cuts up the earth with his plough, and from that earth comes the rich and plentiful harvest. The more a man is chastened, the greater is the harvest of spiritual virtues shown forth by him.[130]

MEN WHO suffer not, attain no perfection. The plant most pruned by the gardeners is that one which, when the summer comes, will have the most beautiful blossoms and the most abundant fruit.[131]

ANYBODY can be happy in the state of comfort, ease, health, success, pleasure and joy; but if one will be happy and contented in the time of trouble, hardship and prevailing disease, it is the proof of nobility.[132]

Reflections
on the Value of Deeds

Fewness of Words,
Abundance of Deeds

T HE ESSENCE of faith is fewness of words and abundance of deeds; he whose words exceed his deeds, know verily his death is better than his life.[133]

O SON of My Handmaid! Guidance hath ever been given by words, and now it is given by deeds. Every one must show forth deeds that are pure and holy, for words are the property of all alike . . .[134]

LET YOUR ACTS be a guide unto all mankind, for the professions of most men, be they high or low, differ from their conduct. It is through your deeds that ye can distinguish yourselves from others. Through them the brightness of your light can be shed upon the whole earth.[135]

O SON of Dust! Verily I say unto thee: Of all men the most negligent is he that disputeth idly and seeketh to advance himself over his brother. Say, O brethren! Let deeds, not words, be your adorning.[136]

LOVE YE all religions and all races with a love that is true and sincere and show that love through deeds and not through the tongue; for the latter hath no importance, as the majority of men are, in speech, well-wishers, while action is the best.[137]

. . . IT IS ACTIONS that speak to the world and are the cause of the progress of humanity.[138]

WELL IS IT with the doers of great deeds.[139]

THOSE WHO do most good use fewest words concerning their actions.[140]

A MAN who does great good, and talks not of it, is on the way to perfection.

The man who has accomplished a small good and magnifies it in his speech is worth very little.[141]

The Importance of Action

D O NOT be content with showing friendship in words alone, let your heart burn with loving kindness for all who may cross your path.[142]

WHAT PROFIT is there in agreeing that universal friendship is good, and talking of the solidarity of the human race as a grand ideal? Unless these thoughts are translated into the world of action, they are useless.[143]

. . . ALL EFFORT and exertion put forth by man from the fullness of his heart is worship, if it is prompted by the highest motives and the will to do service to humanity. This is worship: to serve mankind and to minister to the needs of the people. Service is prayer. A physician ministering to the sick, gently, tenderly, free from prejudice and believing in the solidarity of the human race, he is giving praise.[144]

O MY SERVANT! The best of men are they that earn a livelihood by their calling and spend upon themselves and upon their kindred . . .[145]

O MY SERVANT! The basest of men are they that yield no fruit on earth. Such men are verily counted as among the dead, nay better are the dead in the sight of God than those idle and worthless souls.[146]

Reflections
on Religion

Worship

WORSHIP thou God in such wise that if thy worship lead thee to the fire, no alteration in thine adoration would be produced, and so likewise if thy recompense should be paradise. Thus and thus alone should be the worship which befitteth the one True God. Shouldst thou worship Him because of fear, this would be unseemly in the sanctified Court of His presence, and could not be regarded as an act by thee dedicated to the Oneness of His Being. Or if thy gaze should be on paradise, and thou shouldst worship Him while cherishing such a hope, thou wouldst make God's creation a partner with Him, notwithstanding the fact that paradise is desired by men.

Fire and paradise both bow down and prostrate themselves before God. That which is worthy of His Essence is to worship Him for His sake, without fear of fire, or hope of paradise.[147]

The Purpose of Religion

O YE CHILDREN of men! The fundamental purpose animating the Faith of God and His Religion is to safeguard the interests and promote the unity of the human race, and to foster the spirit of love and fellowship amongst men. Suffer it not to become a source of dissension and discord, of hate and enmity. This is the straight Path, the fixed and immovable foundation.[148]

THE PURPOSE of religion as revealed from the heaven of God's holy Will is to establish unity and concord amongst the peoples of the world; make it not the cause of dissension and strife.[149]

IF RELIGION becomes the source of antagonism and strife, the absence of religion is to be preferred. Religion is meant to be the quickening life of the body politic; if it be the cause of death to humanity, its nonexistence would be a blessing and benefit to man.[150]

RELIGION, MOREOVER, is not a series of beliefs, a set of customs; religion is the teachings of the Lord God, teachings which constitute the very life of humankind, which urge high thoughts upon the mind, refine the character, and lay the groundwork for man's everlasting honour.[151]

ALAS THAT HUMANITY is completely submerged in imitations and unrealities, notwithstanding that the truth of divine religion has ever remained the same. Superstitions have obscured the fundamental reality, the world is darkened, and the light of religion is not apparent. This darkness is conducive to differences and dissensions; rites and dogmas are many and various; therefore, discord has arisen among the religious systems, whereas religion is for the unification of mankind. True religion is the source of love and agreement amongst men, the cause of the development of praiseworthy qualities . . .[152]

The Need for Religion

I F THE EDIFICE of religion shakes and totters, commotion and chaos will ensue and the order of things will be utterly upset, for in the world of mankind there are two safeguards that protect man from wrongdoing. One is the law which punishes the criminal; but the law prevents only the manifest crime and not the concealed sin; whereas the ideal safeguard, namely, the religion of God, prevents both the manifest and the concealed crime, trains man, educates morals, compels the adoption of virtues and is the all-inclusive power which guarantees the felicity of the world of mankind. But by religion is meant that which is ascertained by investigation and not that which is based on mere imitation, the foundations of Divine Religions and not human imitations.[153]

CONSIDER HISTORY. What has brought unity to nations, morality to peoples and benefits to mankind? If we reflect upon it, we will find that establishing the divine religions has been the greatest means toward accomplishing the oneness of humanity. The foundation of divine reality in religion has done this, not imitations of ancestral religious forms. Imitations are opposed to each other and have ever been the cause of strife, enmity, jealousy and war. The divine religions are collective centres in which diverse standpoints may meet, agree and unify.[154]

The Decline in Religion

THE VITALITY of men's belief in God is dying out in every land; nothing short of His wholesome medicine can ever restore it. The corrosion of ungodliness is eating into the vitals of human society; what else but the Elixir of His potent Revelation can cleanse and revive it? Is it within human power . . . to effect in the constituent elements of any of the minute and indivisible particles of matter so complete a transformation as to transmute it into purest gold? Perplexing and difficult as this may appear, the still greater task of converting satanic strength into heavenly power is one that We have been empowered to accomplish. The Force capable of such a transformation transcendeth the potency of the Elixir itself. The Word of God, alone, can claim the distinction of being endowed with the capacity required for so great and far-reaching a change.[155]

RELIGION IS VERILY the chief instrument for the establishment of order in the world and of tranquillity amongst its peoples. The weakening of the pillars of religion hath strengthened the foolish and emboldened them and made them more arrogant. Verily I say: The greater the decline of religion, the more grievous the waywardness of the ungodly. This cannot but lead in the end to chaos and confusion.[156]

GOD HIMSELF has indeed been dethroned from the hearts of men, and an idolatrous world passionately and clamorously hails and worships the false gods which its own idle fancies have fatuously created, and its misguided hands so impiously exalted.[157]

Imaginary Religion

ARISE, O PEOPLE, and, by the power of God's might, resolve to gain the victory over your own selves, that haply the whole earth may be freed and sanctified from its servitude to the gods of its idle fancies – gods that have inflicted such loss upon, and are responsible for the misery of, their wretched worshippers. These idols form the obstacle that impedeth man in his efforts to advance in the path of perfection.[158]

SOME WORSHIP the product of their own imagination: they make for themselves an imaginary God and adore this, when the creation of their finite minds cannot be the Infinite Mighty Maker of all things . . .[159]

The Need for the Renewal of Religion

A LL CONDITIONS and requisites of the past unfitted and inadequate for the present time are undergoing radical reform. It is evident, therefore, that counterfeit and spurious religious teaching, antiquated forms of belief and ancestral imitations which are at variance with the foundations of divine reality must also pass away and be reformed. They must be abandoned and new conditions be recognized. The morals of humanity must undergo change. New remedies and solutions for human problems must be adopted. Human intellects themselves must change and be subject to the universal reformation. Just as the thoughts and hypotheses of past ages are fruitless today, likewise dogmas and codes of human invention are obsolete and barren of product in religion. Nay, it is true that they are the cause of enmity and conducive to strife in the world of humanity; war and bloodshed proceed from them, and the oneness of mankind finds no recognition in their observance.[160]

THE NATIONS and religions are steeped in blind and bigoted imitations. A man is a Jew because his father was a Jew. The Muslim follows implicitly the footsteps of his ancestors in belief and observance. The Buddhist is true to his heredity as a Buddhist. That is to say, they profess religious belief blindly and without investigation, making unity and agreement impossible. It is evident, therefore, that this condition will not be remedied without a reformation in the world of religion. In other words, the fundamental reality of the divine religions must be renewed, reformed, revoiced to mankind.[161]

RELIGION is the outer expression of the divine reality. Therefore, it must be living, vitalized, moving and progressive. If it be without motion and nonprogressive, it is without the divine life; it is dead. The divine institutes are continuously active and evolutionary; therefore, the revelation of them must be progressive and continuous. All things are subject to reformation.[162]

FROM THE SEED of reality religion has grown into a tree which has put forth leaves and branches, blossoms and fruit. After a time this tree has fallen into a condition of decay. The leaves and blossoms have withered and perished; the tree has become stricken and fruitless. It is not reasonable that man should hold to the old tree, claiming that its life forces are undiminished, its fruit unequaled, its existence eternal. The seed of reality must be sown again in human hearts in order that a new tree may grow therefrom and new divine fruits refresh the world. By this means the nations and peoples now divergent in religion will be brought into unity, imitations will be forsaken, and a universal brotherhood in reality itself will be established.[163]

The Unity of Religions

I T IS the outward practices of religion that are so different, and it is they that cause disputes and enmity – while the reality is always the same, and one. The Reality is the Truth, and truth has no division.[164]

. . . RELIGIOUS TRUTH is not absolute but relative, that Divine Revelation is a continuous and progressive process, that all the great religions of the world are divine in origin, that their basic principles are in complete harmony, that their aims and purposes are one and the same, that their teachings are but facets of one truth, that their functions are complementary, that they differ only in the nonessential aspects of their doctrines, and that their missions represent successive stages in the spiritual evolution of human society . . .[165]

Science and Religion

R ELIGION AND SCIENCE are the two wings upon which man's intelligence can soar into the heights, with which the human soul can progress. It is not possible to fly with one wing alone! Should a man try to fly with the wing of religion alone he would quickly fall into the quagmire of superstition, whilst on the other hand, with the wing of science alone he would also make no progress, but fall into the despairing slough of materialism.[166]

ALL RELIGIOUS LAWS conform to reason, and are suited to the people for whom they are framed, and for the age in which they are to be obeyed.[167]

... THE RELIGION which does not walk hand in hand with science is itself in the darkness of superstition and ignorance.[168]

IF RELIGIOUS BELIEFS and opinions are found contrary to the standards of science, they are mere superstitions and imaginations; for the antithesis of knowledge is ignorance, and the child of ignorance is superstition.

Unquestionably there must be agreement between true religion and science. If a question be found contrary to reason, faith and belief in it are impossible, and there is no outcome but wavering and vacillation.[169]

CONSIDER WHAT it is that singles man out from among created beings, and makes of him a creature apart. Is it not his reasoning power, his intelligence? Shall he not make use of these in his study of religion? I say unto you: weigh carefully in the balance of reason and science everything that is presented to you as religion. If it passes this test, then accept it, for it is truth! If, however, it does not so conform, then reject it, for it is ignorance![170]

WHATEVER the intelligence of man cannot understand, religion ought not to accept. Religion and science walk hand in hand, and any religion contrary to science is not the truth.[171]

Reflections
on the New World

The Vision of the New World

THE AGE has dawned when human fellowship will become a reality.

The century has come when all religions shall be unified.

The dispensation is at hand when all nations shall enjoy the blessings of international peace.[172]

. . . ALL NATIONS and kindreds will be gathered together under the shadow of this Divine Banner, which is no other than the Lordly Branch itself, and will become a single nation. Religious and sectarian antagonism, the hostility of races and peoples, and differences among nations, will be eliminated. All men will adhere to one religion, will have one common faith, will be blended into one race, and become a single people. All will dwell in one common fatherland, which is the planet itself.[173]

THE UNITY of the human race, as envisaged by Bahá'u'lláh implies the establishment of a world commonwealth in which all nations, races, creeds and classes are closely and permanently united, and in which the autonomy of its state members and the personal freedom and initiative of the individuals that compose them are definitely and completely safeguarded. This commonwealth must, as far as we can visualize it, consist of a world legislature, whose members will, as the trustees of the whole of mankind, ultimately control the entire resources of all the component nations, and will enact such laws as shall be required to regulate the life, satisfy the needs and adjust the relationships of all races and peoples. A world executive, backed by an international Force, will carry out the decisions arrived at, and apply the laws enacted by, this world legislature, and will safeguard the organic unity of the whole commonwealth. A world tribunal will adjudicate and deliver its compulsory and final verdict in all and any disputes that may arise between the various elements constituting this universal system. A mechanism of world inter-communication will be devised, embracing the whole planet, freed from national hindrances and restrictions, and functioning with marvellous swiftness and perfect regularity. A world metropolis will act as the nerve centre of a world civilization, the focus towards which the unifying forces of life will converge and from which its energizing influences will radiate. A world language will either be invented or chosen from among the existing languages and will be taught in the schools of all the federated nations as an auxiliary to their mother tongue. A world script, a world literature, a uniform and universal system of currency, of weights and measures, will simplify and facilitate intercourse and understanding among the nations and races of mankind. In such a world society, science and religion, the two most potent forces in human life, will be reconciled, will cooperate, and will harmoniously develop. The press will, under such a system, while giving full scope to the expression of the diversified views and convictions of mankind, cease to be mischievously manipulated by vested interests, whether private or public, and will be liberated from the influence of contending governments and peoples. The economic resources of the world will be organized, its sources of raw materials will be tapped and fully utilized, its markets will be coordinated and developed, and the distribution of its products will be equitably regulated.

National rivalries, hatred, and intrigues will cease, and racial animosity and prejudice will be replaced by racial amity, understanding and cooperation. The causes of religious strife will be permanently removed, economic barriers and restrictions will be completely abolished, and the inordinate distinction between classes will be obliterated. Destitution on the one hand, and gross accumulation of ownership on the other, will disappear. The enormous energy dissipated and wasted on war, whether economic or political, will be consecrated to such ends as will extend the range of human inventions and technical development, to the increase of the productivity of mankind, to the extermination of disease, to the extension of scientific research, to the raising of the standard of physical health, to the sharpening and refinement of the human brain, to the exploitation of the unused and unsuspected resources of the planet, to the prolongation of human life, and to the furtherance of any other agency that can stimulate the intellectual, the moral, and spiritual life of the entire human race.

A world federal system, ruling the whole earth and exercising unchallengeable authority over its unimaginably vast resources, blending and embodying the ideals of both the East and the West, liberated from the curse of war and its miseries, and bent on the exploitation of all the available sources of energy on the surface of the planet, a system in which Force is made the servant of Justice, whose life is sustained by its universal recognition of one God and by its allegiance to one common Revelation – such is the goal towards which humanity, impelled by the unifying forces of life, is moving.[174]

Creating the New World

HE TIME must come when the imperative necessity for the holding of a vast, an all-embracing assemblage of men will be universally realized. The rulers and kings of the earth must needs attend it, and, participating in its deliberations, must consider such ways and means as will lay the foundations of the world's Great Peace amongst men. Such a peace demandeth that the Great Powers should resolve, for the sake of the tranquillity of the peoples of the earth, to be fully reconciled among themselves. Should any king take up arms against another, all should unitedly arise and prevent him. If this be done, the nations of the world will no longer require any armaments, except for the purpose of preserving the security of their realms and of maintaining internal order within their territories. This will ensure the peace and composure of every people, government and nation.[175]

LET YOUR VISION be world-embracing, rather than confined to your own self. The Evil One is he that hindereth the rise and obstructeth the spiritual progress of the children of men.

It is incumbent upon every man, in this Day, to hold fast unto whatsoever will promote the interests, and exalt the station, of all nations and just governments.[176]

WHEN RELIGION, shorn of its superstitions, traditions, and unintelligent dogmas, shows its conformity with science, then will there be a great unifying, cleansing force in the world which will sweep before it all wars, disagreements, discords and struggles – and then will mankind be united . . .[177]

MAY FANATICISM and religious bigotry be unknown, all humanity enter the bond of brotherhood, souls consort in perfect agreement, the nations of earth at last hoist the banner of truth, and the religions of the world enter the divine temple of oneness, for the foundations of the heavenly religions are one reality. Reality is not divisible; it does not admit multiplicity.[178]

SO FAR as ye are able, ignite a candle of love in every meeting, and with tenderness rejoice and cheer ye every heart. Care for the stranger as for one of your own; show to alien souls the same loving kindness ye bestow upon your faithful friends. Should any come to blows with you, seek to be friends with him; should any stab you to the heart, be ye a healing salve unto his sores; should any taunt and mock at you, meet him with love. Should any heap his blame upon you, praise ye him; should he offer you a deadly poison, give him the choicest honey in exchange; and should he threaten your life, grant him a remedy that will heal him evermore. Should he be pain itself, be ye his medicine;

should he be thorns, be ye his roses and sweet herbs. Perchance such ways and words from you will make this darksome world turn bright at last; will make this dusty earth turn heavenly, this devilish prison place become a royal palace of the Lord – so that war and strife will pass and be no more, and love and trust will pitch their tents on the summits of the world.[179]

. . . LOVE AND GOOD FAITH must so dominate the human heart that men will regard the stranger as a familiar friend, the malefactor as one of their own, the alien even as a loved one, the enemy as a companion dear and close. Who killeth them, him will they call a bestower of life; who turneth away from them, him will they regard as turning towards them; who denieth their message, him will they consider as one acknowledging its truth. The meaning is that they must treat all humankind even as they treat their sympathizers, their fellow-believers, their loved ones and familiar friends.

Should such a torch light up the world community, ye will find that the whole earth is sending forth a fragrance, that it hath become a delightsome paradise, and the face of it the image of high heaven. Then will the whole world be one native land, its diverse peoples one single kind, the nations of both east and west one household.[180]

Aspects of the New World

THE DAY is approaching when all the peoples of the world will have adopted one universal language and one common script. When this is achieved, to whatsoever city a man may journey, it shall be as if he were entering his own home. These things are obligatory and absolutely essential. It is incumbent upon every man of insight and understanding to strive to translate that which hath been written into reality and action . . . That one indeed is a man who, today, dedicateth himself to the service of the entire human race. The Great Being saith: Blessed and happy is he that ariseth to promote the best interests of the peoples and kindreds of the earth. In another passage He hath proclaimed: It is not for him to pride himself who loveth his own country, but rather for him who loveth the whole world. The earth is but one country, and mankind its citizens.[181]

THE WORLD in the past has been ruled by force, and man has dominated over woman by reason of his more forceful and aggressive qualities both of body and mind. But the balance is already shifting; force is losing its dominance, and mental alertness, intuition, and the spiritual qualities of love and service, in which woman is strong, are gaining ascendancy. Hence the new age will be an age less masculine and more permeated with the feminine ideals, or, to speak more exactly, will be an age in which the masculine and feminine elements of civilization will be more evenly balanced.[182]

SOME FORM of a world super-state must needs be evolved, in whose favor all the nations of the world will have willingly ceded every claim to make war, certain rights to impose taxation and all rights to maintain armaments, except for purposes of maintaining internal order within their respective dominions. Such a state will have to include within its orbit an international executive adequate to enforce supreme and unchallengeable authority on every recalcitrant member of the commonwealth; a world parliament whose members shall be elected by the people in their respective countries and whose election shall be confirmed by their respective governments; and a supreme tribunal whose judgement will have a binding effect even in such cases where the parties concerned did not voluntarily agree to submit their case to its consideration. A world community in which all economic barriers will have been permanently demolished and the interdependence of Capital and Labour definitely recognized; in which the clamour of religious fanaticism and strife will have been forever stilled; in which the flame of racial animosity will have been finally extinguished; in which a single code of international law – the product of the considered judgement of the world's federated representatives –

shall have as its sanction the instant and coercive intervention of the combined forces of the federated units; and finally a world community in which the fury of a capricious and militant nationalism will have been transmuted into an abiding consciousness of world citizenship – such indeed, appears, in its broadest outline, the Order anticipated by Bahá'u'lláh, an Order that shall come to be regarded as the fairest fruit of a slowly maturing age.[183]

Unity in Diversity

O F ONE TREE are all ye the fruit, and of one bough the leaves. Let not man glory in this that he loveth his country, let him rather glory in this that he loveth his kind.[184]

CONSIDER THE FLOWERS of a garden: though differing in kind, colour, form and shape, yet, inasmuch as they are refreshed by the waters of one spring, revived by the breath of one wind, invigorated by the rays of one sun, this diversity increaseth their charm, and addeth unto their beauty. Thus when that unifying force, the penetrating influence of the Word of God, taketh effect, the difference of customs, manners, habits, ideas, opinions and dispositions embellisheth the world of humanity. This diversity, this difference is like the naturally created dissimilarity and variety of the limbs and organs of the human body, for each one contributeth to the beauty, efficiency and perfection of the whole. When these different limbs and organs come under the influence of man's sovereign soul, and the soul's power pervadeth the limbs and members, veins and arteries of the body, then difference reinforceth harmony, diversity strengtheneth love, and multiplicity is the greatest factor for co-ordination.

How unpleasing to the eye if all the flowers and plants, the leaves and blossoms, the fruits, the branches and the trees of that garden were all of the same shape and colour! Diversity of hues, form and shape, enricheth and adorneth the garden, and heighteneth the effect thereof. In like manner, when divers shades of thought, temperament and character, are brought together under the power and influence of one central agency, the beauty and glory of human perfection will be revealed and made manifest.[185]

LET THERE BE no mistake. The principle of the Oneness of Mankind – the pivot round which all the teachings of Bahá'u'lláh revolve – is no mere outburst of ignorant emotionalism or an expression of vague and pious hope. Its appeal is not to be merely identified with a reawakening of the spirit of brotherhood and good-will among men, nor does it aim solely at the fostering of harmonious cooperation among individual peoples and nations. Its implications are deeper, its claims greater than any which the Prophets of old were allowed to advance. Its message is applicable not only to the individual, but concerns itself primarily with the nature of those essential relationships that must bind all the states and nations as members of one human family. It does not constitute merely the enunciation of an ideal, but stands inseparably associated with an institution adequate to embody its truth, demonstrate its validity, and perpetuate its influence. It implies an organic change in the structure of present-day society, a change such as the world has not yet experienced. It constitutes a challenge, at once bold and universal, to outworn shibboleths of national creeds – creeds that have had their day and which must, in the ordinary course of events as shaped and controlled by Providence, give way to a new gospel, fundamentally different from, and infinitely superior to, what the world has already conceived. It calls for no less than the reconstruction and the demilitarization of the whole civilized world – a world organically unified in all the essential aspects of its life, its political machinery, its spiritual aspiration, its trade and finance, its script and language, and yet infinite in the diversity of the national characteristics of its federated units.

It represents the consummation of human evolution – an evolution that has had its earliest beginnings in the birth of family life, its subsequent development in the achievement of tribal solidarity, leading in turn to the constitution of the city-state, and expanding later into the institution of independent and sovereign nations.[186]

The Beauty of the New World

W HAT A BLESSING that will be – when all shall come together, even as once separate torrents, rivers and streams, running brooks and single drops, when collected together in one place will form a mighty sea. And to such a degree will the inherent unity of all prevail, that the traditions, rules, customs and distinctions in the fanciful life of these populations will be effaced and vanish away like isolated drops, once the great sea of oneness doth leap and surge and roll.

I swear by the Ancient Beauty, that at such a time overwhelming grace will so encircle all, and the sea of grandeur will so overflow its shores, that the narrowest strip of water will grow wide as an endless sea, and every merest drop will be even as the shoreless deep.[187]

HEAR ME, ye mortal birds! In the Rose Garden of changeless splendour a Flower hath begun to bloom, compared to which every other flower is but a thorn, and before the brightness of Whose glory the very essence of beauty must pale and wither. Arise, therefore, and, with the whole enthusiasm of your hearts, with all the eagerness of your souls, the full fervour of your will, and the concentrated efforts of your entire being, strive to attain the paradise of His presence, and endeavour to inhale the fragrance of the incorruptible Flower, to breathe the sweet savours of holiness, and to obtain a portion of this perfume of celestial glory. Whoso followeth this counsel will break his chains asunder, will taste the abandonment of enraptured love, will attain unto his heart's desire, and will surrender his soul into the hands of his Beloved. Bursting through his cage, he will, even as the bird of the spirit, wing his flight to his holy and everlasting nest.[188]

Bibliography

'Abdu'l-Bahá. *Foundations of World Unity*. Wilmette, Illinois: Bahá'í Publishing Trust, 1971.

- *Paris Talks*. Oakham: Bahá'í Publishing Trust, 1979.

- *The Promulgation of Universal Peace*. Wilmette, Illinois: Bahá'í Publishing Trust, 1982.

- *Tablets of the Divine Plan*. Wilmette, Illinois: Bahá'í Publishing Trust, 1977.

- *Secret of Divine Civilization*, Wilmette, Illinois: Bahá'í Publishing Trust, 1990.

- *Selections from the Writings of 'Abdu'l-Bahá*. Haifa: Bahá'í World Centre, 1978.

- *Some Answered Questions*. Wilmette, Illinois: Bahá'í Publishing Trust, 1990.

The Báb, *Selections from the Writings of the Báb*. Haifa: Bahá'í World Centre, 1976.

Bahá'í World Faith. Wilmette, Illinois: Bahá'í Publishing Trust, 1971.

BIBLIOGRAPHY

Bahá'u'lláh, *Gleanings from the Writings of Bahá'u'lláh*. Wilmette, Illinois: Bahá'í Publishing Trust, 1983.

- *The Hidden Words*. Wilmette, Illinois: Bahá'í Publishing Trust, 1990.

- *Kitáb-i-Íqán*. Wilmette, Illinois: Bahá'í Publishing Trust, 1950.

- *Prayers and Meditations*. Wilmette, Illinois: Bahá'í Publishing Trust, 1987.

- *The Proclamation of Bahá'u'lláh*, Wilmette, Illinois: Bahá'í Publishing Trust, 1967.

- *The Seven Valleys and The Four Valleys*. Wilmette, Illinois: Bahá'í Publishing Trust, 1991.

- *Tablets of Bahá'u'lláh revealed after the Kitáb-i-Aqdas*. Wilmette, Illinois: Bahá'í Publishing Trust, 1988.

Esslemont, J.E. *Bahá'u'lláh and the New Era*. Wilmette, Illinois: Bahá'í Publishing Trust, 1980.

Shoghi Effendi. *The Promised Day is Come*. Wilmette, Illinois: Bahá'í Publishing Trust, 1980.

- *The World Order of Bahá'u'lláh*. Wilmette, Illinois: Bahá'í Publishing Trust, 1991.

Synopsis and Codification of the Laws and Ordinances of the Kitáb-i-Aqdas. Haifa: Bahá'í World Centre, 1973.

References

Reflections on the Meaning of Life

1. Bahá'u'lláh, *Gleanings*, p. 215.
2. ibid. p. 8.
3. 'Abdu'l-Bahá, *Selections*, p. 161.
4. Bahá'u'lláh, *Gleanings*, pp. 259-60.
5. 'Abdu'l-Bahá, *Paris Talks*, p. 17.
6. ibid. p. 79.
7. ibid. p. 31.
8. 'Abdu'l-Bahá, *Divine Plan*, p. 87.
9. 'Abdu'l-Bahá, *Foundations*, p. 42.
10. ibid. pp. 42-3.
11. Bahá'u'lláh, *Gleanings*, p. 218.
12. ibid. p. 250.
13. 'Abdu'l-Bahá, *Promulgation*, p. 123.
14. Shoghi Effendi, *World Order*, p. 198.
15. 'Abdu'l-Bahá, *Promulgation*, p. 11.
16. Bahá'u'lláh, *Tablets*, p. 71.
17. ibid. p. 64.
18. 'Abdu'l-Bahá, *Paris Talks*, p. 60.
19. 'Abdu'l-Bahá, *Some Answered Questions*, p. 233.
20. 'Abdu'l-Bahá, *Paris Talks*, p. 90.
21. Bahá'u'lláh, *Synopsis*, p. 12.
22. Bahá'u'lláh, *Hidden Words*, Arabic no. 48.

23. 'Abdu'l-Bahá, *Paris Talks*, p. 178.
24. ibid. p. 50.
25. 'Abdu'l-Bahá, *Selections*, p. 120.
26. ibid. p. 24.
27. 'Abdu'l-Bahá, *Paris Talks*, p. 136.
28. 'Abdu'l-Bahá, *Some Answered Questions*, p. 77.
29. ibid. pp. 38-9.
30. Bahá'u'lláh, *Hidden Words*, Persian no. 26.
31. Bahá'u'lláh, *Gleanings*, p. 327.
32. Bahá'u'lláh, *Tablets*, p. 156.
33. ibid. p. 35.
34. 'Abdu'l-Bahá, *Bahá'í World Faith*, p. 410.

Reflections on the Mystery of Love

35. 'Abdu'l-Bahá, *Selections*, p. 27.
36. 'Abdu'l-Bahá, *Promulgation*, pp. 255-6.
37. Bahá'u'lláh, *Gleanings*, p. 96.
38. 'Abdu'l-Bahá, *Paris Talks*, p. 179.
39. 'Abdu'l-Bahá, *Promulgation*, p. 297.
40. ibid. p. 268.
41. Bahá'u'lláh, *Seven Valleys*, p. 7.
42. Bahá'u'lláh, *Hidden Words*, Persian no. 4.
43. Bahá'u'lláh, *Prayers and Meditations*, p. 96.
44. 'Abdu'l-Bahá, *Paris Talks*, pp. 179-80.
45. 'Abdu'l-Bahá, *Bahá'í World Faith*, p. 368.
46. ibid. p. 9.
47. Bahá'u'lláh, *Seven Valleys*, p. 8.
48. ibid. p. 10.
49. ibid. p. 13.
50. Bahá'u'lláh, *Tablets*, p. 36.
51. Bahá'u'lláh, *Gleanings*, p. 250.
52. ibid. p. 218.
53. Bahá'u'lláh, *Hidden Words*, Persian no. 3.

REFLECTIONS

54. 'Abdu'l-Bahá, *Paris Talks*, pp. 29-30.
55. ibid. p. 53.
56. 'Abdu'l-Bahá, *Bahá'í World Faith*, p. 217.
57. 'Abdu'l-Bahá, *Promulgation*, pp. 144-5.
58. ibid. pp. 390-1.
59. 'Abdu'l-Bahá, *Bahá'í World Faith*, p. 356.
60. 'Abdu'l-Bahá, *Selections*, p. 3.
61. ibid. pp. 35-6.
62. ibid. p. 72.
63. 'Abdu'l-Bahá, *Bahá'í World Faith*, p. 353.

Reflections on Peace

64. Bahá'u'lláh, *Gleanings*, p. 218.
65. Bahá'u'lláh, *Tablets*, p. 72.
66. 'Abdu'l-Bahá, *Selections*, pp. 300-1.
67. 'Abdu'l-Bahá, *Promulgation*, p. 119.
68. ibid. pp. 156-7.
69. 'Abdu'l-Bahá, *Paris Talks*, p. 29.
70. ibid. p. 102.
71. ibid. pp. 149-50.
72. 'Abdu'l-Bahá, *Bahá'í World Faith*, p. 284.
73. ibid. p. 428.
74. 'Abdu'l-Bahá, *Promulgation*, p. 123.
75. 'Abdu'l-Bahá, *Selections*, pp. 257-8.
76. 'Abdu'l-Bahá, *Bahá'í World Faith*, p. 240.
77. Bahá'u'lláh, *Tablets*, pp. 138-9.
78. Bahá'u'lláh, *Gleanings*, pp. 6-7.
79. 'Abdu'l-Bahá, *Paris Talks*, p. 29.
80. 'Abdu'l-Bahá, *Selections*, p. 282.
81. 'Abdu'l-Bahá, *Bahá'í World Faith*, p. 230.
82. ibid. p. 244.
83. ibid. p. 356.
84. 'Abdu'l-Bahá, *Paris Talks*, p. 43.

85. ibid.
86. ibid. p. 115.
87. 'Abdu'l-Bahá, *Selections*, p. 26.
88. Bahá'u'lláh, *Gleanings*, p. 140.
89. ibid. p. 217.
90. 'Abdu'l-Bahá, *Bahá'í World Faith*, p. 268.
91. 'Abdu'l-Bahá, *Promulgation*, pp. 31-2.
92. 'Abdu'l-Bahá, *Bahá'í World Faith*, p. 258.
93. 'Abdu'l-Bahá, *Promulgation*, p. 265.
94. Bahá'u'lláh, *Gleanings*, pp. 253-4.
95. 'Abdu'l-Bahá, *Secret of Divine Civilization*, p. 71.
96. ibid. pp. 64-6.

Reflections on Virtue

97. Bahá'u'lláh, *Tablets*, p. 36.
98. ibid. p. 257.
99. 'Abdu'l-Bahá, *Paris Talks*, p. 113.
100. 'Abdu'l-Bahá, *Some Answered Questions*, p. 144.
101. Bahá'u'lláh, *Hidden Words*, Arabic no. 1.
102. Bahá'u'lláh, *Gleanings*, p. 285.
103. 'Abdu'l-Bahá, *Selections*, p. 273.
104. ibid. p. 271.
105. 'Abdu'l-Bahá, *Promulgation*, pp. 14-15.
106. 'Abdu'l-Bahá, *Selections*, p. 245.
107. Bahá'u'lláh, *Gleanings*, p. 215.
108. Bahá'u'lláh, *Tablets*, p. 88.
109. Bahá'u'lláh, *Proclamation*, p. 20.
110. Bahá'u'lláh, *Kitáb-i-Íqán*, p. 3.
111. 'Abdu'l-Bahá, *Selections*, pp. 303-4.
112. 'Abdu'l-Bahá, *Paris Talks*, p. 87.
113. Bahá'u'lláh, *Gleanings*, p. 203.
114. ibid. p. 204.
115. 'Abdu'l-Bahá, *Divine Plan*, p. 23.

116. Abdu'l-Bahá, *Selections*, p. 256.
117. Bahá'u'lláh, *Gleanings*, p. 315.
118. Bahá'u'lláh, *Hidden Words*, Arabic no. 2.
119. 'Abdu'l-Bahá, *Some Answered Questions*, p. 137.
120. 'Abdu'l-Bahá, *Promulgation*, p. 84.
121. Bahá'u'lláh, *Tablets*, p. 143.
122. ibid. p. 72.
123. ibid. p. 37.
124. ibid. p. 40.
125. 'Abdu'l-Bahá, *Selections*, p. 136.
126. Bahá'u'lláh, *Gleanings*, p. 81.
127. Bahá'u'lláh, *Tablets*, p. 66.
128. ibid. p. 171.
129. Bahá'u'lláh, *Hidden Words*, Persian no. 36.
130. 'Abdu'l-Bahá, *Paris Talks*, p. 51.
131. ibid.
132. 'Abdu'l-Bahá, *Bahá'í World Faith*, p. 363.

Reflections on the Value of Deeds

133. Bahá'u'lláh, *Tablets*, p. 156.
134. Bahá'u'lláh, *Hidden Words*, Persian no. 76.
135. Bahá'u'lláh, *Gleanings*, p. 305.
136. Bahá'u'lláh, *Hidden Words*, Persian no. 5.
137. 'Abdu'l-Bahá, *Selections*, p. 69.
138. 'Abdu'l-Bahá, *Paris Talks*, p. 80.
139. 'Abdu'l-Bahá, *Selections*, p. 267.
140. 'Abdu'l-Bahá, *Paris Talks*, p. 17.
141. ibid. p. 16.
142. ibid.
143. ibid.
144. ibid. pp. 176-7.
145. Bahá'u'lláh, *Hidden Words*, Persian no. 82.
146. ibid. no. 81.

Reflections on Religion

147. The Báb, *Selections*, pp. 77-8.
148. Bahá'u'lláh, *Gleanings*, p. 215.
149. Bahá'u'lláh, *Tablets*, p. 129.
150. 'Abdu'l-Bahá, *Promulgation*, p. 117.
151. 'Abdu'l-Bahá, *Selections*, pp. 52-3.
152. 'Abdu'l-Bahá, *Promulgation*, p 179.
153. 'Abdu'l-Bahá, *Selections*, pp. 302-3.
154. 'Abdu'l-Bahá, *Promulgation*, p. 158.
155. Bahá'u'lláh, *Gleanings*, pp. 199-200.
156. Bahá'u'lláh, *Tablets*, pp. 63-4.
157. Shoghi Effendi, *Promised Day is Come*, pp. 113-14.
158. Bahá'u'lláh, *Gleanings*, p. 93.
159. 'Abdu'l-Bahá, *Paris Talks*, p. 145.
160. 'Abdu'l-Bahá, *Promulgation*, p. 144.
161. ibid. p. 141.
162. ibid. p. 140.
163. ibid. pp. 141-2.
164. 'Abdu'l-Bahá, *Paris Talks*, pp. 120-1.
165. Shoghi Effendi, Statement prepared by him in 1948 for the United Nations Special Palestine Committee, *Promised Day is Come*, p. v.
166. 'Abdu'l-Bahá, *Paris Talks*, p. 143.
167. ibid. pp. 141-2.
168. ibid. p. 144.
169. 'Abdu'l-Bahá, *Promulgation*, p. 181.
170. 'Abdu'l-Bahá, *Paris Talks*, p. 144.
171. ibid. p. 131.

Reflections on the New World

172. 'Abdu'l-Bahá, *Promulgation*, p. 370.
173. 'Abdu'l-Bahá, *Some Answered Questions*, p. 65.

174. Shoghi Effendi, *World Order*, pp. 203-4.
175. Bahá'u'lláh, *Gleanings*, p. 249.
176. ibid. pp. 94-5.
177. 'Abdu'l-Bahá, *Paris Talks*, p. 146.
178. 'Abdu'l-Bahá, *Promulgation*, pp. 95-6.
179. 'Abdu'l-Bahá, *Selections*, p. 34.
180. ibid. p. 84.
181. Bahá'u'lláh, *Gleanings*, pp. 249-50.
182. 'Abdu'l-Bahá quoted in Esslemont, *New Era*, p. 149.
183. Shoghi Effendi, *World Order*, pp. 40-1.
184. Bahá'u'lláh, *Tablets*, pp. 127-8.
185. 'Abdu'l-Bahá, *Selections*, pp. 291-2.
186. Shoghi Effendi, *World Order*, pp. 42-3.
187. Abdu'l-Bahá, *Selections*, pp. 260-1.

End Piece

188. Bahá'u'lláh, *Gleanings*, pp. 320-1.

Personal Reflections

Personal Reflections

Personal Reflections

Personal Reflections

Personal Reflections

Personal Reflections

BEST STORIES

FOR

SEVEN YEAR OLDS

Also available from Hodder Story Collections

- Best Stories for Under Fives

- Best Stories for Five Year Olds

- Best Stories for Six Year Olds